THE INHABITANTS
Photographs and Text by Wright Morris
Second Edition

"I guess a look is what a man gets not so much from inhabiting something as from something that's inhabiting him. Maybe this is what it is that inhabits a house. In all my life I've never been in anything so crowded, so full of something, as the rooms of a vacant house. . . . Sometimes I think only vacant houses are occupied. . . . An Inhabitant is what you can't take away from a house. . . ."

With the publication of **THE INHABITANTS**, Wright Morris opened new horizons in the relationship between photographs and words. His portraits of fragments of America, caught untenanted, suggested the people who had built, lived in, handled, wasted, loved, and eventually abandoned the time- and weather-worn buildings that fascinated him. All that remained was to supply the people—to deduce from what remained, the identities of those who had come and gone.

This beautiful book is the result of his vision—a poignant landscape of Middle America of the thirties and forties; of the rapidly vanishing agrarian heartlands of Morris' boyhood and the voices of the people they belonged to. In the text, Morris has captured the verbal style and the inner spirit of men and women on the move. Their outlook and their dreams unite with the pictures to form an evocative portrait of America. Each exists independently, until joined in the mind's eye of the reader.

"**THE INHABITANTS** was published . . . in 1946. For more than twenty years it has been out of print and steadily escalating on the rare book market. Time has revealed that American life of the thirties gave rise to new visions of American experience that were peculiarly the province of the photographer. This book is one, and I am gratified to see it made available to a new generation of readers, possibly more inclined than their elders to take a close look at both the facts, and the artifacts."—*From the Preface*

THE
INHABITANTS

THE INHABITANTS

Second Edition

Text and Photographs by
WRIGHT MORRIS

DA CAPO PRESS   New York · 1972

The Inhabitants was originally published by Charles Scribner's Sons, New York, in 1946. For this second edition, the author has prepared a preface and has replaced two photographs (plates 17 and 48) that appeared in the original edition. In all other respects, this Da Capo Press edition is an unabridged republication of the first edition.

Copyright, 1946, by Charles Scribner's Sons
Copyright © 1971 by Wright Morris

Published by Da Capo Press, Inc.
A Subsidiary of Plenum Publishing Corporation
227 West 17th Street, New York, New York 10011

Library of Congress Cataloging in Publication Data

Morris, Wright, 1910—
    The inhabitants.

    1. United States—Social life and customs—1918-
1945—Pictorial works.   2. United States—Description
and travel—Views.   3. Architecture—United States—
Pictorial works.   I. Title.
EL169.M88   1972   917.3   70-115681
ISBN 0-306-71931-2

All Rights Reserved.

Printed in United States of America

PREFACE TO THE SECOND EDITION

In the spring of 1935 I stopped work on the fiction I was writing to buy a camera and take some pictures. The prints that I made and enlarged impressed me as somewhat peculiar. What did I propose to do with a portrait of the incinerator at the back of the yard? Or several loose boards in the fence along the alley? These were followed by views of a decaying porch and several highly prized shots of a neighbor's privy, with a close-up of the door. Was it the texture, perhaps? Photographers were known to be interested in texture. Apparently I had more than texture in mind on the evidence of the subjects I assembled. Doors and windows, gates, stoops, samples of litter, assorted junk, anything that appeared to have served its purpose. Except people. Only in their absence will the observer intuit, in full measure, their presence in the object.

As the prints accumulated, and as the photographer looked about for subjects, it was clear that what he sought were facts of a sort—artifacts. Expressive fragments that managed to speak for the whole. This was also being done by other searchers, such as archaeologists, who could dig up, or assemble from the fragments, the thing itself. My interest paralleled that of such diggers, but even when found, the-thing-itself must be encouraged to speak. In the matter of selection of such objects, I relied entirely on my feelings about them: They spoke to me or they did not speak. Behind my eyes, in the complex of my nature, I had a reliable Geiger counter. When exposed to radiant raw material, it ticked.

The artifacts I selected from the great quantity present proved to be those that indelibly revealed the hand of man. Not so much the *handi*work as the work that is largely shaped by experience—it is the nature of *this* experience that *this* artifact reveals. Meaningful things, as we say. I was focused on those meaningful to me. I was free to exclude "people" from this search, since people, as I knew them, were the subject of my fiction, and I found them—or failed to find them—through the effort and discipline of writing.

My writing of that time testifies to a similar obsession with "things." It is frequently tormented in striving to get the simple word to fit the simple object. That was what I wanted. As much as possible of the *ding an sich*. Hardly a mystery then, being a young man of my time, aware of such a remarkable tool as the camera, that I should use one in an effort to salvage what I valued. I use the word salvage advisedly. We turn our backs—no more—and the valued object is gone. This experience has become so commonplace that nostalgia itself is a diminished emotion. How long will it be before it lacks objects on which to feed?

In admitting to the role that the available past plays in my selection of meaningful objects, I do no more than admit to what I value in experience, and seek to repossess.

More than fifteen years would pass from my first groping snapshots to my first reading of James' *The American Scene*, where he flawlessly articulates what was obscure in my own motives. In his words, I am "subject to the superstition that objects and places, disposed for human use and addressed to it, must have a sense of their own, a mystic meaning proper to themselves to give out. . . ." These words speak directly to what my photo-text books are about.

I first had the idea of combining photos and text following a summer of work on Cape Cod. I wanted each media to exist independently—until joined in the mind's eye of the reader. No illustrational ties. If anything, quite the contrary. To make certain no misleading ties are formed, or suggested, *The Inhabitants* is stubbornly unrelenting on the nature of the photo-text union. I relaxed from these elevated standards later, feeling the point of interest to me had been made. I have heard from readers distracted by the photos, and from lookers distracted by the reading, each testifying, inadvertently, to the separate faculties it is the intent of the book to join.

It was of interest to me, in reviewing the volume, that it contains several photos taken the first year I used a camera. They are of a piece with the photos taken fifteen years later. They show the same preoccupation with time-worn artifacts, and an impulse to impose some aesthetic order. In *The Inhabitants* the elements of design frequently take precedence over the subject matter (as in plate 20), shaping it to an abstract statement. The tendency to stand, in Thoreau's words, "right fronting and face to face to a fact", often reveals in the subject, as well as in my taste, elements that are surprisingly classical. It is a vision of marble imposed on more vulnerable, ephemeral materials, soon gone with the wind.

The Inhabitants was published by Charles Scribner's Sons in 1946. For more than twenty years it has been out of print and steadily escalating on the rare book market. Time has revealed that American life of the thirties gave rise to new visions of American experience that were peculiarly the province of the photographer. This book is one, and I am gratified to see it made available to a new generation of readers, possibly more inclined than their elders to take a close look at both the facts, and the artifacts.

Mill Valley, California   WRIGHT MORRIS
December 1969

FOR

THE INHABITANTS

Who know what it is to be an American

What of architectural beauty I now see, I know has gradually grown from within outward, out of the necessities and character of the indweller, who is the only builder—out of some unconscious truthfulness, and nobleness, without ever a thought for the appearance and whatever additional beauty of this kind is destined to be produced will be preceded by a like unconscious beauty of life . . . it is the life of the inhabitants whose shells they are . . .
                                                            Thoreau

Love consists in this,
that two solitudes protect,
and touch, and greet each other.
                                        Rilke

Thoreau, a look is what a man gets when he tries to inhabit something —something like America.

Take your look—from your look I'd say you did pretty well. Nearly anybody would say you look like a man who grew up around here—but I think I'd say what there is around here grew up in you. What I'm saying is that you're the one that's inhabited.

I guess a look is what a man gets not so much from inhabiting something, as from something that's inhabiting him. Maybe this is what it is that inhabits a house. In all my life I've never been in anything so crowded, so full of something, as the rooms of a vacant house. Sometimes I think only vacant houses are occupied. That's something I knew as a boy but I had nobody to tell me that that's what an Inhabitant is. An Inhabitant is what you can't take away from a house. You can take away everything else— in fact, the more you take away the better you can see what this thing is. That's how you know—that's how you can tell an Inhabitant.

It's getting harder than ever to tell what an American is —

There was a time there was more than room enough for everybody, it was there to be had, it didn't have to be made. But in my time what room there is has to be made. In my time a solution of topsoil is something more than muddy water, and a river of it is more than a river is meant to be. The Big Muddy is something more than a river's name. In my time the Land can be seen from nearly all of our great bridges—flowing beneath, a rich solution of America. Landscapes creating seascapes everywhere. And as to what an American is nearly any man can tell you—I can give you the answer of the American who lives here.

He says an American is a man who minds his own goddam business— you can see for yourself that he's minded it goddam well. That in his own terms he's a dam good American.

But easier and easier to tell an Inhabitant.

All he ever heard was wagon wheels in the dust somewhere. Every night was a Saturday night and everything he saw had the look things have when a band is passing by. All he ever saw in people was what they were meant to be. And I think what he thought they were meant to be was something to love. I tell you I've never seen a man so much in love. When we were sitting in the square what he saw wasn't the same people, wasn't the same streets, for all I know wasn't the same town. Just to sit there with him made everything softer, like a secret was around. What he saw wasn't the people so much as something over the people, like the smell of leaves burning or the dust that hangs over the square. Like the harvest moon, he saw everything bigger than it really was. I can't tell you what he saw—but I can tell you it was something he could love.

My people grew up around here and they've got some of that look about them — and some of that talk, they look and talk about the same.

He was lyin' there. Willie, I said, why the hell ain't you up loafin'? Then I looked an seen he was dead. Now Willie must've died mid-winter 'cause the tree he had through the window wasn't anymore than half burnt. Willie burnt just one tree a year. He'd prop it through the window with one end in the stove and push on it now and then when it burnt. And there he was. One leg was hangin' with the boot half laced and a piece of the lace was still in his hand. The law said he died tryin' to get that boot off. But anyone who knew Willie could see he was tryin' to get it on. But he wasn't goin' anywhere. Willie'd allus vowed that he was a man who was goin' to die with his boots on—but I reckon he didn't vow it as much as he should. For the Lord come callin' right when he had 'em off and he must've stood knockin' at the door. But Willie wunt one to rush for any man.

You hear talk of a man finding himself — seems to me I can find myself anywhere. There's a big piece in Willie — and a small piece in Mordecai.

I guess what there was of Mordecai was mostly in God. Willie liked his right to be left alone and Mordecai liked his right to come and butt in—sounds contrary, but it's the same man, top and bottom side. Willie used to say that anything that would cover him and Mordecai would cover everything—and where there was room for the likes of them there was room for us all.

Well, maybe there was—anyhow that's what Willie used to say.

There's some of it in Charlie —

Here I come
Hello Charlie
How's tide?
Low Charlie
How's scallops?
Fine Charlie
Bye now
Bye Charlie
Here I go.

And some of it in Uncle John.

My cane has the carved head of a dog, smooth hollow sockets are his eyes. Walking, I keep my fingers there. I can feel him check me at a rise and lead me where objects fall away. Space is a thing we lean upon. We can feel my son's new love affair as he stoops and tips my head to shave. My wife's patience rises from her hair. We can read a storm and hear a color glow, and in the rain we can smell a sparrow's fear. But to see, they say, is a thing we do not know.

What is there between the branch and the apple when it falls?

We have seen it—we would recognize it anywhere. Yet of an evening we are told nothing is there.

Then there's some pieces left over I've never really looked into.

I can see it comin'—one of these days there's going to be a law makin' it illegal for a man to have a hard time. Any man who has a hard time they'll tell you is just a little bit looney—they'll pass a law to keep him off the streets. There'll be people whose job it is to put an end to your hard time, or see about puttin' an end to you. Now bygod, Mister, if it ain't hard times, if it ain't honest troubles that make a man, I'd like to know just what in the hell it is? When you take away troubles you got to know what to take away. Instead of troubles maybe you take away the man. I'm not tellin' you how it should be, I'm just tellin' you how it is—I'm tellin' you things you like are different than things you love. Mister, you can't just like a thing with the hard-times label on it—you either hate it, or you think its somethin' to love. Seems to me we're pretty well agreed that this is sure one hell of a world— but what about the one they tell me is comin' up? What about the pretty world I see every week in the magazine ads? In that wonderful place I've seen a lot of things a man might fancy, things he might like, but not a dam thing that he could love. Bygod, you'd swear that after all there's been, after years of stuff that would freeze hell over, that people would have a good idea what Hell is. Seems to me we still got no idea of it at all. Seems to me, Mister, Hell is a place where there's never no more real troubles, where people are happy because there's never no more hard times. A nice little place where you get what you like—and not what you love.

I guess Grandpa got away first — he just picked up and headed for Kansas — but the thing about Grandpa is that all you see is where he is from. No matter where he is all you see is where he is from —

I remember him leavin' his oatmeal with the sugar meltin' on it and walkin' out to where the privy stood. Then he come in and sit messin' with his spoon. Then he said, Ma—I'm goin' to build it on the rise. She turned from the stove and looked at him, then she looked away, and he got up and left his oatmeal just sittin' there. Through the window we seen him cross the yard and look off at the rise like the house was already built and the shingles on. And like he was standin' there in the door he waved to us. He's a damned old fool, I said—that wind'll blow you clean to hell—but I could see that what was growin' on him was growin' on her. And she just sat and looked at him like at a litter of new pups.

That's all you see about Grandma —
As a matter of fact Grandma didn't leave. Grandpa just more or less kid-
napped her.

She took the change from the glass sugar bowl and gave it to him. She held his vest while he put it on, then she buttoned it up. There was a stripe in the vest and she said that he looked good in a stripe. There was none of it left where he sat or bent at the knees. She made him blow at her like at a match, and she backed away. She dipped a toothpick in wintergreen oil and made him chew on the end until she didn't blink when he said *Ah!* There was a stripe in his coat except where it bent at the sleeve. There was a chain with a gold toothpick in a case like a sword. Then he put the sugar bowl change in his pocket but she made him take it out and put it in his vest where it belonged.

But it's not all you see in their kids —
Or maybe you do — maybe Will was what Grandpa had in mind. It was
clear what he should do, and from what I've seen I'd say that he did it —

Donaldson's hitch bar would have to go. So would the split elm and the horse trough full of marbles, the old chain swing. Mr. Cole said the horses would soon go too. Cement paving would wear their hooves to the bone, he said. Willie said, for what did horses have shoes? Mr. Cole spit and said some day the paving would go right out of town. It would go to the east first, and then it would go to the west. He said when Willie had kids he'd bet their kids would ride it for miles. And when their kids had kids they'd ride it clear to Omaha. Willie rolled up his sleeve and felt in the horse trough for marbles. What makes you think, Willie said, that I'm goin' in for kids?

But it was not so clear for Anna —

She came in with the eggs and he came in with the milk. She held them like clothespins in her apron and with her thumb nail scratched off the hen spots. He picked up *Capper's Weekly* and sat down to take off his shoes. He put his socks to dry out in the cob bin, turned up the lamp. She sat on the rocker near the stove and when she rocked her high button shoes came unbuttoned and the lumps in her stockings showed. He held out his hand and she pulled from her head a long gray hair. He stretched it over the lamp chimney and when it singed he turned down the wick. What was left of the hair he handed back to her. He read, but she didn't care to read. She rocked and wound her hair around and around her finger and looked at the picture of her mother on the wall. Everybody said how much it was they were just alike. Everybody knew she had worked right up till the day she died.

Nor so clear for me —
My Dad and me weren't so much alike — then again I sometimes think we were. He just came first, and after doing what he did — I had to come.

When I was a kid I saw the town through a crack in the grain elevator, an island of trees in the quiet sea of corn. That had been the day the end of the world was at hand. Miss Baumgartner let us out of school so we could go and watch it end, or hide and peek at it from somewhere. Dean Cole and I walked a block and then we ran. We ran all the way to the tracks and down the tracks to the grain elevator, through the hole in the bottom and up the ladder inside. We stretched on our bellies and looked through a crack at the town. We could see all the way to Chapman and a train smoking somewhere. We could see the Platte beyond the tall corn and the bridge where PeeWee dived in the sand, and we could see T. B. Horde driving by with his county fair mare. We could see it all and the end of the world was at hand.

The end of the world! I said.

HOO-RAY! said Dean Cole.

And after doing what I did — that is, what I didn't — I guess Evelyn had to come.

Kiss me—she said.

It's bad.

I don't mind.

You'll have your drawin' an your name in a backhouse and if your name's you then ain't you a backhouse?

Kiss me—she said, and her eyes were soft closed and he couldn't breathe, couldn't run, couldn't nothin' and she made kissing sounds and when she did it again why he just reached over and slapped her. He slapped her smart-like and the noise scared her awake and except for one spot she was white as a leghorn, but where he had slapped was like the skin of an apple and she turned and ran off down the road.

I don't know whether Dwight had to come or not—
But when he came he found the Lord waiting and everything around him
Heaven-sent.

He sent the night as Sandman to the sun and the great sky sea for sailing off to Nod and the cradle moon to rock the baby stars and the peep-hole nights to dream behind the sea and—

More?

And he made Center City and the candy case at Eoff's and the crawl holes under porches and the extra crust on pies and—

More—?

And tar all oozy-goozy and the gummy-gum on trees and the drawers for thing-ma-doodles and garter snakes and little boys—

But not little girls! he said.

Oh goodness no!

Then she came and everything around him went to hell.

When her birthday came it was out on the lawn with colored lights and Japanese lanterns and blindfolded people wondering where to pin the donkey's tail. The Baptists drove by slow in their buggies but some of the Methodists stopped and came in. When there were too many she shot her Roman candles at them. I got sick and had to go to bed early so she brought me her birthday cake, saying that I was to blow out the candles for her. But there were only eight more candles on hers than there'd been on mine. I couldn't blow—all I could do was watch them burn. She sat on the bed in the new fur coat my father had given her and she asked me if I thought I was old enough to kiss her good night. I said it wasn't me that wasn't old enough, but that it was her. She didn't say anything and nobody blew the candles out. They burned right down and sputtered in the icing on the cake. Through the window we watched my father climb the tree and take down the lanterns and then walk around picking up the cups and paper plates. When he was through he called for her, but she didn't come. She sat on the bed till I fell asleep and I thought she was still there in the morning, but it was only her rumpled birthday coat.

Seems like when you start with something like Grandpa you end up with something like Mitchell —

Let's see now—there's Will, an there's Anna, an there's Paul, an then there's—

Uncle Toby?

An then there's Toby, an there's Clara, there's Maude—let's see now, that's seven, now who would be eight? As sure as God made little apples we was eight—

There's you Uncle Mitchell!

Why bless me—so there is. Let's see now, there's Will, Anna, Paul, an Toby, there's Clara, Maude—an then there's . . .

You—

Umhmmh—there's me.

Or something like Paul.

He was a little man but I remember him big. He had arms like a Christmas stocking and he held them out like his hands were wet, wet and dripping and like he had to keep them away. He was like a firecracker that had gone funk somewhere. It was lit when you tossed it away but it didn't go off, it didn't even sputter—the fuse looked dead but it was fizzing inside somewhere. There was something about him like spit-on carbide in an air tight can. He would wait to go off until you got close to him, had him right in your hand.

*And when you start with something like Grandma you end up with some-
thing like Toby —
Uncle Toby thought he'd go back where it all came from.*

Lady—I said—if it's bait you want I got it, if it's Beach Plum jelly you want I got it, an if it's sass you want—well, I got that too. And what'd she say? She said wonderful—what a charactur. Seems to me we're just a breedin' ground for charactur. Anyhow, Lady—I said—it's people like you comin' here that's makin' old fools outa men, and men outa old fools. There's more char-actur, I said, in the side of that house—and I pointed at it—than there is in any old fool you'll find around here. And what'd she say? She said wonderful—what a charactur! And what'd I say? Lady—I said—I'm inclined to agree you're right.

What had come out with the men seemed to end up, somehow, with the women —

She piled the plates and passed the toothpick box. The men leaned back and scratched their matches under the chairs. They looked through the window at the cob pile and the brown-sacked corn.

That was good pie, said Bane.

That was right good pie, said Dill.

They watched her pour water into the dishpan, stir up the suds. The cats came in from the cob pile and mewed at the screen.

You men stayin' in the kitchen? she said.

We ain't really dressed for callin', said Dill.

They turned to watch her open the screen and empty the pan. The cats sniffed at the wet spot from the edges but the chickens tracked in. She hooked the screen and took the lamp from above the sink. They watched her move through the door, after a while heard her sag in the chair.

That was right good pie, said Bane.

It sure was, said Dill.

And the women — ?
Well, they seemed to end up with the men.

She wiped the table with the dish rag then leaned there, propped on her spread arms. A few leaves rattled in the yard. Some dirty leghorns clucked and waited at the screen. She left the rag on the table and emptied the pan toward the leaky shade. She stood there awhile, her hands pressed into the small of her back. Turning, she looked down the trail bright now with copper leaves at an old man's knees, white in the sun. She watched his brown hands lift Monkey Ward's, tear out a page. She watched him read both sides, very slowly, then tip his head. As he rose his overalls came up with a sigh and one strap hung swinging between his legs. She watched him step into the sun and hook it up. From his hat he took a feather and passed it through the stem of his pipe, then turned to strike the match on the door.

I might have ended up myself if it hadn't been for Martha Lee. She left with the paving — the paving went east, so she went east too. Sometimes I wonder if there had been no paving, nothing leaving, if she would have stayed. If she had stayed — chances are I would still be there.

Shadows are the way things lay-me-down. Daddy can lay-me-down across the street. Mr. Clarke's store can lay-me-down on the barn and the barn can lay-me-down on Mr. Clark. Everything that stands up must lay-me-down. The fence, tracks in the road, birds that fly low, poles, trees, myself. Everything tall must lay-me-down like everything short. Everything hard as flat as everything soft. Everything loud as quiet as everything still. Even birds know why and have to lay-me-down too. Even the night must come and lay-me-down to sleep.

Some men put up with the paving leaving, the women leaving, even the rain — but when the land itself started leaving they had to give up.

Never forget how the old man kept his hair. Eighty some, but don't think he lost a hair. Dam near everything else, but he kept that. And he went right on thinking that he kept the land. He'd been on it sixty-five years and right to the last he refused to sell it—but how in the hell you keep it from blowing away? We couldn't get him to move, he'd play like he was deaf and we couldn't budge him. All we could do was sneak a little food in the house and leave him there. Then one day I found him hitching himself up to the plow. There he was, standing there in the harness, and bygod he was stone blind. I tell you he went blind rather than see that land blow away. He had to eat it, had to breathe it, but bygod he refused to watch it blow. Well—what's left is mine, but I can't bring myself to sell or to live on it. I can't get over the feeling that the old man is still there.

They went east, and east means Chicago. And the east goes west to Chicago —

I was a young fella, lookin' at shoes in an army store. In the winda I seen a woman passin', an she was big, an I like big women, an there she was out walkin' a little fice of a man. She looked at me an I looked back at her. I was a free man and I needed a woman—so what did I do? I stood there lookin' at the shoes in the army store. She walked him slow givin' me time, stoppin' at everything she could stop at, an I was a free man, I'd been lookin' an waitin'—so what did I do? I looked once—that's all I did, just looked at her. Then I seen my own face in the window lookin' at me. Now bygod it looked like a man, it looked like a man's face front and side—but there wasn't a man inside to make it talk. If I'm a free man I'd like to know what the hell I'm free for? But never mind, I've had it pretty well explained to me. When I was a young fella I took it pretty hard. Now I see that what's free is like the gum you get on the corner—before you learn it ain't good manners to spit it out. Well, I've been chewin' that stuff nearly ten, fifteen years. That's why it is you hear so much talk how the flavor lasts. But no need to tell me—an I guess there's not much need to tell you.

What people aren't there are young people going —

There 'leven of us—I the might-be Lincoln one. So I come heah. My daddy say Lincoln some man up heah. Well, I heah. I heah—but I still the might-be one.

Or old people gone.

Some call it fire, some call it murder—what does it matter what you call it when you sit up in bed, your eyes wide, and hear it go by? You sit up in bed and wonder if next time it'll be for you. Every town has a smell a little bit different than the next town, a smell of its own, but they all got the same cry in the night. That's what you hear when you sit up in bed and forget to lie back—or maybe you walk in the bathroom and have a good look at your face. That's what you hear, and that's what you see in your face. When a man died they used to ring bells, but when men die like they do in the city, bells aren't much use—you need something that people can hear. You need something to scream at you in the night. You need something that says everything unsaid about you, what you never dared say to your neighbors, or to yourself. You need something that says all of that in just one word, just one shriek, and that's what we got. So long as we got that sound we know how it is each with other, we know we're all lonely, we know we're like kids scared to death. And knowing it is better than just lying there. Some call it fire, some call it murder, some call it just an accident, Mister. Then there's some who don't call it—they listen. They know what it is.

You can find anything in Chicago —
Robin Hood, he's there —

Men—we gotta act fast. When he comes ridin' we gotta be set—see yur gats is loaded an tripped. See ya gotta fresh slug in yur mitt. Spike you go leak an eye on the road, an men—

Who's tha bloke? said Spike.

Trigger McSorley let his gat droop. Razor Scarlatti peeled his sword from his fly.

Who tha hell are *you?* said Spike.

He spit.

You tha Green Hornet?

HA! he said.

You tha Lone Ranger?

He spit again.

Then who?

Me—? I'm Robin Hood, he said.

And Mrs. Mulligan is there —

Mr. Mulligan met her in Duluth. Her name was Ola Lindgren then and she was out in a boat. When her time was up it was Mr. Mulligan's boat. And what did she do but fall in getting out. And what did he do but jump in just like he was. He saved her and then they went home together to dry off. Oh my, oh my, and then his pants wouldn't go on. They were married in Minneapolis where he went to have his teeth out. Oh my, in Duluth she liked to sit with the ear phones on and watch it get dark or go barefoot and leave talcum footprints on the linoleum. None of that in Salt Lake City or Omaha, none of that here. First came Joey and two little brothers even stronger than he was. Then Louie, then the government let him die in the pest house. Last Christmas Olie Lindgren sent them some real fur gloves. Next Christmas they would send him something.

You can find anything in Chicago because everything tends to end up there. I know boys who both began — and ended there.

The woman lay quiet on the mattress. An el went by and he felt it with his body. A street car passed and he felt that too.

Get goin' Guagliardo!

Domenic, Benito and Kovak. Domenic stood up and buttoned his pants and his dice fell out on the mattress.

Get goin'—! said the woman.

She raised her knees and made a sound with her skirts and he felt that too with his body. What a fine thing he had for a body. What did he hear when he felt things and what did he feel when he heard them? Domenic was telling him where to get off. Kovak was telling him something. He watched Domenic stoop for a rock and felt Domenic find it. No use trying to duck Domenic. The woman got up and made sounds with her clothes and they all walked out on Blackhawk. Domenic had hit him too high for his teeth. Benito would hit him again.

A boy can't help where he begins anymore than he knows where he is going. And where do you go when the signs don't point anymore?

A kid is a kid because he's what he is in little pieces. He's all broken up like a jigsaw loose in its box. He's just what we make of him and we never make more than we can use, we do what we can to try and make less. Whoever uses the pieces left over, or tells him they're there? Whoever tells him that he was born with the whole of a man somewhere in him, but that half of him is never fitted, scattered on the floor? How is he to know when he's living in hell that heaven is also part of him—not something he gets when he's gone, but has while he's here? How is he to know when the men who fit him are just half men? They don't even know that fitting kids is what a man is for. They don't even know that what a man's dreamed any kid can dream and some can aspire to—they don't even know that what a man's been any kid might be. And they don't seem to know that a kid is more than a man is. To get men you subtract—to get kids you add up the whole damned works.

Where do you go except back where you came from?
I can't tell you how many people have lost track of where they were going
— how many people are not too sure of where they are from.

Dear Son—Have moved. Have nice little place of our own now, two-plate gas. Have Chevrolet 28, spare tire, wire wheels. Crazy to be without it, now get out in country, get out in air. Have extra room, wouldn't be so crowded, nice and quiet in rear. Nice warm sun there every morning, nice view in rear. Have plan to sell day-old eggs to high class Restaurants, Hotels. Soon send you to Harvard—send you to Yale. Saw Robin in yard this morning. Saw him catch worm.

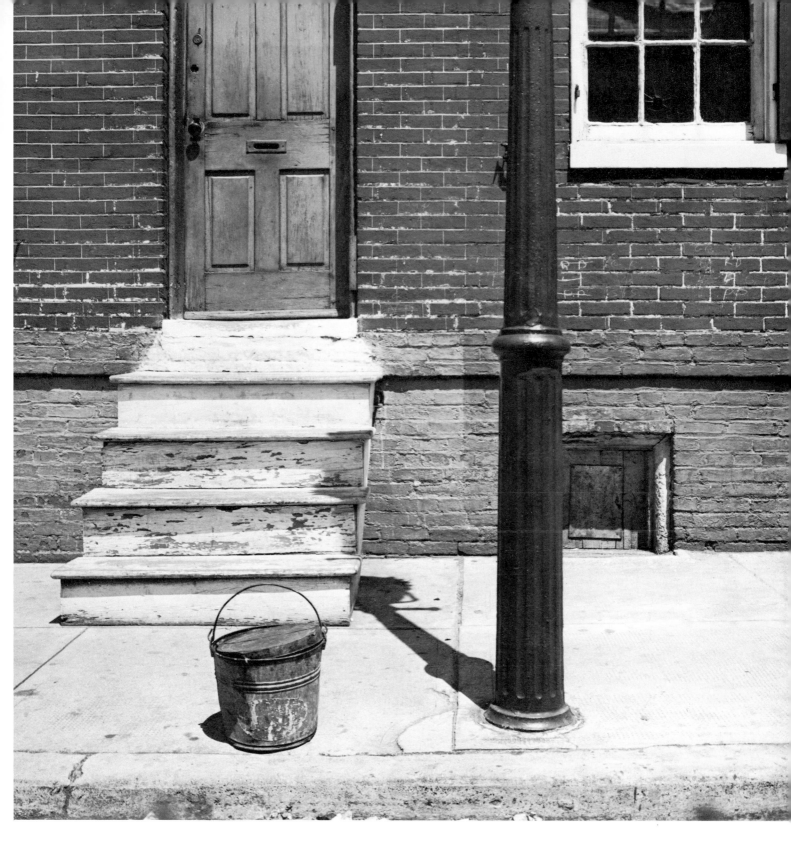

But I can tell you that it's a farm or a little town — and that little towns are mighty big places to be from. The smaller they are the bigger they are to be from —

Through the vines was Bickel's General Store and a brown dog drinking at the fountain. Sparrows dropped from the trees to the wires and then from the wires to the ditch grass. A pigeon dropped from the belfry to the roof of the barn. He went along the tin roof to the hole, dropped inside. Jewel's Tea Wagon passed and the dust came up and went by. More sparrows dropped from the wires, stirred the grass near the road. Mrs. Riddlemosher stopped picking currants and turned with her pan. Mrs. Willard came and stood at the screen. Behind the feed store Mr. Cole's mare whinnied and Mr. Bickel smoothed his apron, stopped shooing flies. Tipping her sunbonnet back Mrs. Riddlemosher looked toward the square where the dust came marching down the road with the rain.

But they never get big enough to hold all the men that left them — the roads lead back, but the travel is still the other way.

I have here, said the man—some beautiful handmade flowers.
He picked one up from the top of the suit box, sniffed at it.
I have just forty-two cents, I said.
It's a quarter, he said.
It's worth forty-two, I said.
The lilies, he said, are worth a dollar.
I put my hand out for the quarter one but the man gave me the lily.
I want the other one, I said.
I'm giving you this one, he said.
I've only forty-two cents, I said.
I'm *giving* you this one, he said.
Now listen—I said.
I can give it too, he said.
Now listen here—I said.
I'm not a beggar, he said.
Of course not, I said, you're in business.
It's slow, he said, but it's a business.
But business, I said, is business—
I'm giving you this one, he said.
Well, thank you very much—I said.
I can give it too—he said, and walked away.

There's a Pied Piper in every big town that draws a man there. Sometimes I think what a man hears is the city stalled like an engine, her fires banked, and some of her power leaking out in the air. What my Dad thought he heard — guess I thought I heard it too. I guess we were so much alike that what was done couldn't be done over —

All the same. The streets, the stores, the faces, the people—all the same. An all-over-more something added and that was all. More people, more big, more everything, more less at home. More the less alone it seemed the more he was. More people to know than he'd ever dreamed, more people seen than he'd ever know, more left unsaid. All people in windows, not people you come to know. A girl in a window showing a ring or holding a bottle and tapping the glass, or stripped down some showing even more. Or a man with a corset to melt your pouch or if you hadn't a pouch it would widen your shoulders, lengthen your life. Nobody thought of talking to her or seeing more than the pouch on him, or wondering if whoever they were they were alive. They were just the pouch, or the ring, or the look, or whatever they did. Not somebody to know or like but something to buy. Something to have if you first just had the dough.

But I thought I could leave it — yes sir, that was what I thought.
That was what I thought until I met Abby. Washington D.C. is the home of
Abby.

This is how it is—
There's them who find it so hard they get all-over tough. There's them who find it harder and they get all-over soft. Then there's them who just plain find it hard. All I got to say to them is look at me. All they got to say to me they already said. And that's all there is to people, got it all in myself. Them who don't find it hard just ain't people—they somethin' else.

That was what I thought until I met Furman Young.
Hard to say where Furman's home is — or where it ain't.

I've come to see the land is here for spreadin' me on. Never been in Ox Bow or Wahoo, never been in Wagon Mound or Steamboat Springs, but I can tell you I'm there—there's part of me there right now. Never owned a house or a piece of land, never owned a woman, no kid is mine—but maybe I'd rather make talk like this than a family. Like when I tell you, though I don't own it, the land is mine. And if you ask me what kind of land that is, I'll tell you that too. Mister, the land is that part of me I can't leave behind. When I hear the name Corn Hill I see it, or the name Bowling Green, Tombstone, or Lone Tree—and when I hear it I see myself waitin' there for me. Hellsfire, Mister, there was a time all I thought a man did was unravel—now I see that all he does is wind himself up. Where I've been is somethin' but it's nothin' beside where I've yet to go.

Hard to say whether PeeWee Canby lives in New Mexico — or Vermont.

I'd let them grasshoppers spit right in my hand and then rub the juice in my hair for luck—and I got it—one summer I found a two dollar bill. I did, yes sir, I did—but then I lost it before I could spend it, there wasn't anyone in that dam fool town who would believe it was mine. Oh my, and when I think of the Chautauqua, more dam buggies than I'd ever seen an full of women with the popcorn burner sparkin' their eyes. And after the show there was the big boys and the girls. I'd hide in the ditch grass and hear them girls giggle and make little cries. And when it was over bygolly I'd stand and look at the grass. Just stand there like a dam fool kid and stare at the grass. Sometimes it was still warm, like a buckboard seat to the palm of your hand, and I would sit there—like I'm doin' now—and think how it was.

There's a woman named Bronson in Colorado —
She went out in a wagon but she took the east with her — she took some-
thing bigger than any covered wagon would hold.

It was no use to tell her there was rockin' chairs where she was goin'—
no use at all, until her first baby came along. Then she had to choose between
her rockin' chair and the cradle, so she gave up the chair. She gave up the
chair but she didn't give up the seat. She sat up all one night just to unravel
the cane bottom seat. And from then on she wore that cane like it was a life
preserver, all of it wrapped around her waist like a belt. When a snow trapped
them in the Rockies she let them burn everything they had, cradle and all,
except the Bible and that dam cane. Then in the spring I was born and after
she wrote my name in the Bible I think the very next thing she did was work
on a chair. Spend all of her spare time puttin' that old seat in a new chair.
Eight more of us, besides me, grew up sittin' on it. First our names in the
Bible then our bottoms on that chair. I used to think there was something
crazy about how she held on to that cane, and the trouble she had bringin'
it and the family Bible through. But I've learned that her home didn't need
anymore to furnish it. That little piece of cane was a line that she stretched
across the country ahead of both the telephone and the telegraph. And it kept
her in touch with more important things. Between the Bible and that chair
she had room for whatever happened, and she kept our heads in the one
and our bottoms where they belonged.

A man named Pafko a day's ride south —

That thing in your hand there, Buddy, you call that your Freedom from Want? Freedom from Want—now that's a nice name for a dinner pail. That's about the nicest name yet when you think how some of these names don't wear well—all these isms tend to get out of date. But here you've got a really nice American name. You go into a cutrate drugstore and say, Give me one of them gold-plated Freedoms from Want—give me one of them swell American Dreams. Bygod, Buddy, you live in a wonderful time. There's a plague in the world as if people were sick with Freedom, but it's a lovesickness, so they go right on calling for it. We're sick in the heart—but we think we're sick in the dinner pail. And when a man can't tell the difference between his guts and his Freedom—it isn't his dinner, Buddy, it's his gravy he's got in mind. It's gravy, not hunger, that makes men sick like this. How much gravy you find on the men from Buchenwald? Hunger makes a man sick in his flesh but gravy makes him sick where you can't cure him; he loves his sickness, he don't want to be cured. With that kind of sickness more gravy is all he wants. Freedom from Want! Buddy—seems to me you already got it. Seems to me you got it when you don't want Freedom anymore.

And in New Orleans there's something I can't give a name.
For the thing about Abby and the thing about Furman, the thing about those
with names and those without them, is that no name can cover the ground.
You can't cover something like that with a name at all.

A girl with a moist blonde face, her lips parted, peeling like a fresco, pulled at his sleeve and asked—*Did he fall?* Was that what heights were for—places from which to fall? Was there no one to say that someone intended to rise? That he stood there, looking, not to see a man fall but to see a man rise? To see what he had never seen before? *Well, I guess I missed it*, she said, and turned away. That is clear, it is clear that they both missed something. He turned to look for it under a small flowered hat, the face open, the arm trailing a black net shopping bag. She seemed to think that something had happened there. She seemed to see it happening before her eyes. Why didn't he tell her that he had seen nothing fall, nor nothing rise—why did he say what he said to her face?

Madam, he said, *a slight man with a light grey beard and a silk umbrella just stepped from the porch and rose to God.*

That is all—that is all that he said. Then he saw that they were alone, the dead center where the words had dropped like a stone, the crowd rippling off, breaking on the curb.

No matter where you go or what you call it, once you've got this thing you've got it —

He wanna go—but he doan wanna kill no one. He jus wanna help, but he say if he help he gotta go. But he look an walk so sidesaddle I jus doan know. It break his heart to learn he doan walk right. He allus been so proud of his walkin', so relaxed like. Like he say, he can go on an on—all he need is time. An Mister Yancey be so sad to see him go. He so honest for a black man Mister Yancey say. He say he jus' can't unahstan how he black as bottom side of a stove lid an yet so white-like in all his ways. He allus say it when Luke aroun' to make him glad. But now he say some pennies he drop jus' doan come back. I doan know—maybe Luke jus' tired of pickin' 'em up. Or maybe he jus' foun' out what all them pennies is for. Soften the ache he get when he hear how sidesaddle he grown.

Once you've known this thing you can't leave it behind.

Seems to me I've seen about all there is of people, right here, and we're not as many people as you think. I'd say there's just two kinds of people that run around with all of our faces, and there's room for just one face at a time. The other faces have to take a seat in the rear. The one on the front is the one we like to think is a pretty sharp likeness of the face we usually wear around. We give it a name and say it's the face of our time. We give it a name and tell people how close it is we're related, and sit around picking our teeth while they tell us. We tell them, but most of this talk we swallow back down. We swallow it down the same way we dam up the rivers and let just a little trickle of water through. Pretty soon we got more water behind than you'd ever guess from a look at the front. More behind than the front is meant to hold. Then one day—pretty quick-like—we got a new face. A new face—not a new kind of people—like I said there's just two kinds of people. There's the people you know, and then there's the people you don't.

The red man has it —

Under the awning of the Governor's building sit the squaws of five pueblos, the braves stand about bonfires in the street. They are gathered here to honor the World Premier of *The Santa Fe Trail*. Errol Flynn and an all-star cast in *The Santa Fe Trail*. Where he walked can still be seen in the blue slush along the sidewalk, and where he has gone a covey of ladies bar the view. For the white man's Fiesta the squaws have brought pottery and blankets, drawings of the Thunder Bird, and small framed paintings in sand. Julian Martinez, the pottery maker, stands by the fire. He wears a black top-coat and the long braids of his hair are invisible on the black satin lapels. He has seen the Niagara Falls, the Empire State building, the Mammoth Cave, and Fords come off of the assembly line. There is only one great American thing he has not seen. And now this thing, this Hollywood, has come to him. For this was the end—as advertised—of the Santa Fe Trail.

The black man has it —

What if I come to see one killin' make two men dead? I believe I right, he believe he right, but one place we right at same time. Killin' change a man by makin' him dead, that's all. Nothin' else change except more people make more people dead. I say killin's hard, I say dyin's harder—but I say livin's hardest yet. Anybody likely to die for somethin', take a man live it out. Dyin' hurt bad once, livin' hurt bad every day. Every day have to get up, be killed, an' die all over again. Take a good thing make a man put up with somethin' like that. Take a good man to put up with a good thing.

And a lot of people not heard from have it — and to call a man red, black or white doesn't cover the ground. No matter what color he had when he started this new color is the same — and no matter where you go you can't leave it behind.

I told them.

You poor bastards, I said, what the hell have you got, what is yours for working, what the hell do you get for slaving, for being alive? I've seen your lungs, I said, and they're black as a sponge for cleaning stove lids, and out in the sun I've seen you stumble like it was dark. Maybe you're men, I said, but who the hell would know? Men can talk, I said, what the hell have you got to say?

Back under the lantern an old man put up his hand.

Is my lungs black? he said.

Black as hell, I said, they're black as your hands.

The old man held them up to the lantern and looked at his hands in the light.

And I wouldn't have known—he said, I wouldn't have known.

So what—? I said.

I'm grateful to you—he said, smiling—because I wouldn't have known. I came here to learn, he said—an so I did.

There never was a people who tried so hard — and left so little behind as we do. There never was a people who traveled so light — and carried so much.

On the buckboard seat of the wagon, stiff but not quite erect, a woman sits with her hands crossed in her lap. A man is on the seat beside her—beside her but not with her—he is there with the reins but the woman sit alone. He sits crouched, the reins drawn in as if to dull some pain in his belly, turning his head only when he spits on the road. She looks neither to the right nor the left, but sometimes at her hands. She is wearing a print dress with a lace effect at the collar and a few creases at the openings for her arms. A bow draws it in at the waist but everywhere else it puffs away, as if full of wind that nothing would squeeze out. A pattern of flowers grows up and down her frame as on wall paper.

On her head is a small straw hat. It is pink straw with a soft crown in which there are five or six wax cherries, in the band are two feathers and a flower of some kind. The flower is paper, but the feathers are real Plymouth Rock.

Everywhere you look there is a man leaving something — or something that a man left. And everywhere you look you see that nobody left anything.

Long division problems were still on the board. The gold stars for not being tardy were still on the wall. The front row of seats and the hook for the bell, the desk with long pants and the rack for the maps, the Civil War and Harper's Ferry still where they had been. In the back was Orville and up front was Mike, then Pauline he'd kissed and Betty he hadn't, and Jane who wrote long letters to Santa Claus. Where were they now and how had he forgotten? LaRue who drew horses and Irene who danced and Opal who married a married man? Was so much of him somewhere unremembered that what remained had grown even less? Was he every day leaving something behind and was that part of him now bigger than he was? All that he'd touched, seen, known, but knew no more. And if what he had been was really what he was—what was he now? Here in the seat she had sat in braiding up her hair.

This thing a man can't leave behind is America.

Why I do thees theeng? Every theeng else she been done. Every theeng else somewhere, sometime she been done better—better sing, better dance, better look, an a much better love. But theese theeng no time, nowhere, been done at all. Thees theeng got to be done right here. Thees theeng only theeng anywhere left to be doing—thees theeng only theeng left to be for. I do thees theeng or every theeng she fold up. I do thees theeng because she got to be done.

It doesn't matter where he got it, where he takes it, or where he tries to leave it —
If he can't escape it, he's an Inhabitant.

People living elsewhere think they will find it living here. People coming here give up looking for it and go home. People living here don't seem to know anything was lost. What rain there is washes what you think there is away. People coming here get to looking pretty faded—or pretty dark. Whatever you are at bottom you get to be more everyday. But if you can live with it alone and like it—maybe you'll find it here.

I said a look is what a man gets when he is inhabited by something.

In the mirror he could see the slab of the wall and the small table with the Bible—a Gideon Bible with the raw red stain on the leaves. There was a path from the table to where he sat on the bed. He raised his feet and the rug beneath was worn to strands of burlap, the loose strings caulking the cracks in the floor. Did they come here to sleep—those who came here—or to walk between the bed and the table, between the bed and the Book with the raw red stain on the leaves? As if they wondered what the Book was for. As if there was something about a Hotel room and a Gideon Bible—as if the connection, some kind of connection, wasn't clear. As if a long distance call had something very vague about it, the message garbled, but ringing one number all night long. As if the connection had to be made by waiting, waiting and walking—walking the carpet between the front and the back of the mind. For there was something about a bedroom, a carpet and a Gideon Bible, when the connection, the answer, was up to him.·

You can see for yourself —

Revolution? Seems to me that's where we come in. I guess some people think that's where we go out. Seems to me we all like to think that what was done was done forever, the revolution leaving us free to do pretty much as we like. Putting last things first is what we like. We're pretty good now at laying the wreath, holding the flag, raising the mortgage, swearing allegiance and saying the last shall be first. We're so good that I just don't know—I don't know how to tell you, how to tell anybody, what it is that really comes first. Even the revolution doesn't come first. Before the flag and before the mortgage, before the allegiance and laying the wreath—before all that a man named Columbus has to come first. For the revolution is to discover America.

What it is to be an American.

There's no one thing to cover the people, no one sky. There's no one dream to sleep with the people, no one prayer. There's no one hope to rise with the people, no one way or one word for the people, no one sun or one moon for the people, and no one star. For these people are the people and this is their land. And there's no need to cover such people—they cover themselves.